The Juicing and Smoothie Recipe Book

Copyright © 2019 Mary June Smith All Rights Reserved.

No part of this publication may be reproduced, distributed, or transmitted in any form or by any means, including photocopying, recording, or other electronic or mechanical methods, or by any information storage and retrieval system without the prior written permission of Smith Show Publishing, except in the case of very brief quotations embodied in critical reviews and certain other noncommercial uses permitted by copyright law.

Table of Contents

The Pumpkin Shake Smoothie   37

The Peachy Green Smoothie   72

The Trifecta: Mint, Melon, Mango Smoothie   107

What is juicing?

By definition: extract the juice from (fruit or vegetables).

I'm sure by now most of us have heard of juicing in some form or another. Juicing is a process of stripping away the solid matter from fruits and vegetables, leaving behind a glass of liquid goodness. What remains is a juice that contains all of the vitamins and minerals our bodies need. By juicing fruits and vegetables it is quick and easy for our body to digest and assimilate nutrients. Also, juicing helps detox our body because we are consuming a large amount of nutrients in a small volume.

Equipment

When it comes to juicing, you basically have 3 options:
Cold-Pressed, Centrifugal, or Masticating.

Cold-Pressed
This is the absolute best equipment to have. Cold-pressed juicing involves pressing to release the juice. In doing so you get more juice and more nutrients that are retained. No heat or chopping chopping is involved. The downside to this method is the equipment is expensive.

Masticating
Masticating is the next best option. This method grinds which squishes the juice from fruits and veggies. Due to the low speeds there is less heat than the Centrifugal juicers so you retain more juice and nutrients. This type of juicer may also be used to make nut milk, including almond milk.

Centrifugal
If you've looked at juicers at your local box stores, odds are it was a Centrifugal juicer. This juicer spins at high speeds which can cause some heat that leads to nutrient loss. It is suggested that you re-juice (run the fruits and veggies through twice) to have a better yield of juice and reduce waste.

Cleansing Juices

The Honeydew Cucumber
SERVES 2

Ingredients:
1 Medium cucumber
2 cups Kale
¾ cup honeydew melon

Directions:
Add ingredients to juicer alternating between cucumber, kale and honeydew. This ensures you'll leave less behind in the juicer.

The Beetroot Combo
SERVES 2

Ingredients:
1 large beet, scrubbed, halved
4 cups baby spinach
½ Fuji apple, cored
Dash of Nutmeg or Cinnamon (optional)

Directions:
Add all ingredients to juicer alternating between the ingredients being sure to end with fleshy fruits. Pour into a glass and whisk in nutmeg or cinnamon.

The Kale & Beet Cleanser
Serves 2

Ingredients:
2 medium beets, scrubbed, halved
4 cups Kale
1 medium cucumber
¼ lemon
¼ teaspoon cinnamon

Directions:
Add all ingredients to juicer, alternating between the ingredients. Serve in a glass with cinnamon whisked in.

The Refreshing Strawberry Watermelon Smoothie
SERVES 2

Ingredients:
1 cup unsweetened almond milk
1 cup frozen strawberries
1 cup watermelon
1 tablespoon fresh basil
1 cup ice

Directions:
Add the ingredients to a blender and blend until it reaches a smooth texture.

The Watermelon Quencher
SERVES 2

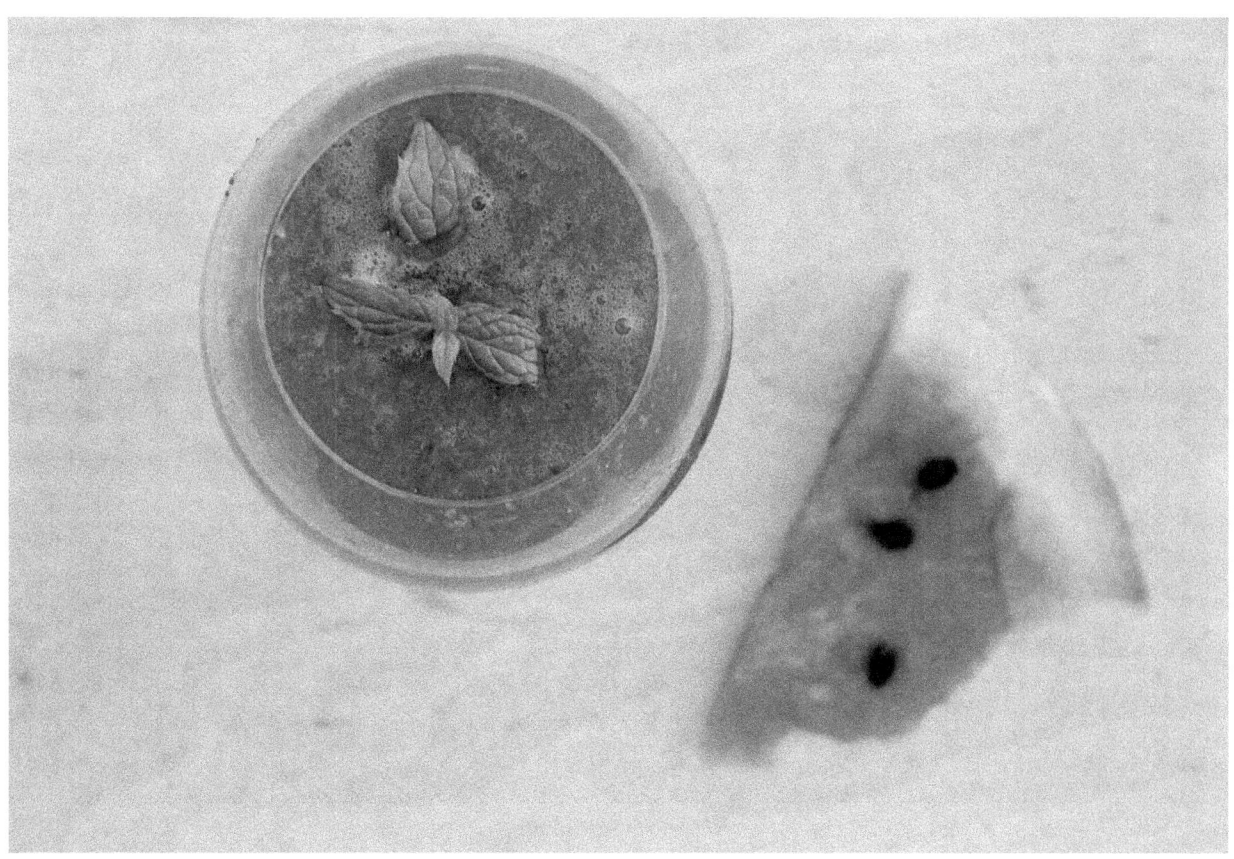

Ingredients:
4 cups watermelon
1 cup baby spinach
1 cup kale
1 large cucumber

Directions:
Add ingredients to the juicer alternating between each of them.

The Cucumber Refresher
SERVES 2

Ingredients:
1 Fuji Apple, quartered
2 cups kale
1 large cucumber

Directions:
Add ingredients alternating between Apple and Kale and Cucumber and Kale being sure to end with Apple or Cucumber.

The Apple Pucker
SERVES 1

Ingredients:
½-¾ head romaine lettuce
3 cups baby spinach
½ Fuji or Granny Smith apple
1 teaspoon fresh ginger (optional)
1 tablespoon lemon juice

Directions:
Add ingredients to juicer alternating between them. Pour into chilled glass and whisk in lemon juice.

The Dandelion Detox Smoothie
SERVES 2

Ingredients:
1 cup unsweetened almond milk
2 cups dandelion greens
1 cup pineapple
1 cup ice

Directions:
Add ingredients into blender and blend until mixture becomes smooth.

The Blueberry Smoothie
SERVES 4

Ingredients:
2 cups coconut water
2 cups baby spinach
2 cups frozen blueberries
½ frozen banana
2 tablespoons spirulina
1 cup ice (optional)

Directions:
Add all ingredients to blender and blend until smooth.

Peaches and Cream Smoothie
SERVES 2

Ingredients:
1¼ cups unsweetened almond milk
1 cup Greek or coconut yogurt
2 cups baby spinach
2 cups frozen peaches
½ frozen banana
1 tablespoon spirulina

Directions:
Add all ingredients to blender and blend until smooth.

The Dark Pumpkin
SERVES 4

Ingredients:
1 cup unsweetened almond milk
1 cup organic pumpkin puree
3 cups baby spinach
½ Bartlett pear, cored
¼ frozen banana
2 tablespoons organic unsweetened cocoa powder
1 tablespoon maple syrup (optional, to taste)
¼ teaspoon pumpkin spice
1 cup ice

Directions:
Add all ingredients to blender and blend until smooth.

The Chocolate Shake Smoothie
SERVES 4

Ingredients:
1cup unsweetened coconut milk
2 cups baby spinach
½ frozen banana
2tablespoons unsweetened cocoa powder
1 tablespoon green superfood
1 tablespoon pure maple syrup
1 cup ice

Directions:
Add all ingredients to blender and blend until smooth

The Cucumber Honeydew Cleanser
SERVES 2

Ingredients:
1 cup coconut water
1 cup honeydew melon
2 cucumbers
1 tablespoon fresh mint
1 cup ice

Directions:
Add all ingredients to blender and blend until smooth.

Morning Boost Juices

The Sweet Melon Kale
SERVES 1

Ingredients:
4 cups kale
1 cup honeydew melon
1 medium cucumber
1 tablespoon lemon juice

Directions:
Add all ingredients to blender except lemon juice. Pour into a chilled glass and whisk in the lemon juice.

The CinnaBeet
SERVES 1

Ingredients:
2 cups baby spinach
1 cup kale
1 medium beet, scrubbed, halved
1 medium cucumber
¼ teaspoon cinnamon

Directions:
Add all ingredients to juicer except cinnamon. Pour into a chilled glass and whisk in cinnamon.

The Beetroot Sun
SERVES 2

Ingredients:
5 cups baby spinach
2 stalks celery
1 medium beet, scrubbed, quartered
¼ Bartlett pear, cored
¼ lemon sliced

Directions:
Add all ingredients to juicer and juice, being sure to alternate the ingredients.

The Raspberry Mint Invigorator Smoothie
SERVES 2

Ingredients:
1 ½ cups unsweetened almond milk
2 cups frozen raspberries
½ frozen banana
1 tablespoon fresh mint
1 teaspoon probiotics
1 cup ice

Directions:
Add all ingredients to blender and blend until smooth.

The Chocolate Wake Up Call Smoothie
SERVES 2

Ingredients:

1 cup unsweetened almond milk

1 cup baby spinach

1 frozen banana

2tablespoons unsweetened cocoa powder

1 tablespoon green superfood

2 tablespoons protein powder

1 cup ice

Directions:

Add all ingredients to blender and blend until smooth.

The Hawaiian Smoothie
SERVES 4

Ingredients:
1 ½ cups unsweetened almond milk
¾ cup pineapple
1 cup frozen mango
1 tablespoon shredded coconut
1 cup ice

Directions:
Add all ingredients to blender and blend until smooth.

The Strawberry Mango Sunrise Smoothie
SERVES 4

Ingredients:

1 ¾ cups unsweetened coconut milk drink

1 cup baby spinach

1 cup frozen strawberries

1 cup frozen (or fresh) mango

4 tablespoons protein powder

1 cup ice

Directions:

Add all ingredients to blender and blend until smooth.

The Green Tea Smoothie
SERVES 4

Ingredients:
1 ½ cups coconut water
2 cups baby spinach
1 frozen banana
2 teaspoons matcha green tea powder
1 teaspoon bee pollen
1 cup ice

Directions:
Add all ingredients to blender and blend until smooth.

The Super Green
SERVES 2

Ingredients:
2 medium Granny Smith apples
2 medium carrots, scrubbed
1 cucumber
15 green grapes
1 medium sweet green pepper
2 cups baby spinach
1 medium whole tomato

Directions:
Add all ingredients to a juicer and juice.

The Green Good Morning Smoothie
SERVES 2

Ingredients:
- 1 cup unsweetened almond milk
- 2 cups baby spinach
- 1 frozen banana
- ½ Fuji apple
- 1 tablespoon green superfood
- 1 tablespoon spirulina
- 1 cup ice

Directions:
Add all ingredients to blender and blend until smooth.

The Breakfast Fusion Smoothie
SERVES 3

Ingredients:
2 cups unsweetened almond milk
2 cups baby spinach
1 ½ cups frozen blueberries
1 frozen banana
¼ cup green superfood
1 teaspoon spirulina
1 cup ice

Directions:
Add all ingredients to blender and blend until smooth.

Cool Satisfying Juices & Smoothies

The Revitalizing Kale Apple
SERVES 1-2

Ingredients:
4 cups kale
1 Fuji apple
1 large cucumber
¼ lemon (optional)

Directions:
Add all of the ingredients in a juicer and juice.

The Purifying Dandelion Pineapple
SERVES 2

Ingredients:
1 ½ cups fresh pineapple
2 cups dandelion greens
2 cups baby spinach
1 ½ cups coconut water

Directions:
Add all of the ingredients to the juicer except the coconut water. Whisk in the coconut water before serving.

The Pumpkin Shake Smoothie
SERVES 2

Ingredients:
1 ½ cups unsweetened almond milk
¾ cup organic pumpkin puree
1 frozen banana
½ Bartlett pear, cored
¼ teaspoon pumpkin spice
4 tablespoons (1 scoop) protein powder
½ cup ice

Directions:
Add all of the ingredients to a blender and blend until smooth.

The Green Vanilla Shake Smoothie
SERVES 2

Ingredients:
1 cup unsweetened coconut water
2 cups baby spinach
1 frozen banana
2 tablespoons almond butter
2 teaspoons organic vanilla extract
4 tablespoons (1 scoop) protein powder
1 cup ice

Directions:
Add all of the ingredients to a blender and blend until smooth.

The Sexy Banana Smoothie
SERVES 4

Ingredients:
1 cup unsweetened almond milk
1 cup baby spinach
1 ½ frozen bananas
2 tablespoons almond butter
4 tablespoons (1 scoop) protein powder
1 cup ice

Directions:
Add all of the ingredients to a blender and blend until smooth.

The Chocolate Peanut Butter Delight Smoothie
SERVES 3

Ingredients:
1 cup unsweetened almond milk
2 cups baby spinach
1 frozen banana
½ Bartlett pear, cored
2 tablespoons natural peanut butter
2 tablespoons unsweetened cocoa powder
1 cup ice

Directions:
Add all of the ingredients to a blender and blend until smooth.

Peaches n' Green Smoothie
SERVES 4

Ingredients:
1 ¾ cups unsweetened almond milk
2 cups baby spinach
½ cup kale
1 tablespoon green superfood
½ frozen banana
2 cups frozen peaches
1 teaspoon spirulina
4 tablespoons (1 scoop) protein powder

Directions:
Add all of the ingredients to a blender and blend until smooth.

The Tart Romaine
SERVES 1

Ingredients:
1 head romaine lettuce
1 Granny Smith apple
½ lemon or lime

Directions:
Add all of the ingredients to the juicer and juice.

The Blueberry Shake Smoothie
SERVES 2-4

Ingredients:
2 cups unsweetened almond milk
1 frozen banana
2 cups frozen blueberries
4 tablespoons (1 scoop) Protein Powder
1 cup ice

Directions:
Add all of the ingredients to a blender and blend until smooth.

The Minty Green Banana Smoothie
SERVES 4

Ingredients:
1 cup unsweetened almond milk
3 cups baby spinach
1 frozen banana
4 tablespoons (1 scoop) protein powder
3 tablespoons mint
2 tablespoons flaxseeds
1 cup ice

Directions:
Add all of the ingredients to blender and blend until smooth.

The Green Clean Smoothie
SERVES 3

Ingredients:
1 ½ cups unsweetened coconut milk drink
2 cups kale
1 frozen banana
1 tablespoon spirulina
2 tablespoons chia seeds
1 cup ice

Directions:
Add all of the ingredients to a blender and blend until smooth.

The Green Beast Smoothie
SERVES 3

Ingredients:
1 cup coconut water
4 cups baby spinach
¾ Bartlett pear, cored
½ Fuji apple
1 teaspoon green superfood
1-2 tablespoons lemon juice, to taste
1 cup ice

Directions:
Add all of the ingredients to a blender and blend until smooth.

The Kale Beauty Potion
SERVES 4

Ingredients:
1½ cups unsweetened coconut milk drink
1 ½ cups kale
2 tablespoons green superfood or spirulina
½ frozen banana
2 Bartlett pears, cored
1 cup ice

Directions:
Add all of the ingredients to a blender and blend until smooth.

The Blue Almond Smoothie
SERVES 4

Ingredients:
2 cups unsweetened almond milk
1 cup baby spinach
1 cup kale
2 cups frozen blueberries
3tablespoons almond butter
2 tablespoons chia seeds

Directions:
Add all of the ingredients to a blender and blend until smooth.

The Dandelion Shake Smoothie
SERVES 2-3

Ingredients:
1 ½ cups unsweetened coconut milk drink
½ cup dandelion greens
2 cups baby spinach
1 frozen banana
3 dried dates, pitted
1 cup ice

Directions:
Add all of the ingredients to a blender and blend until smooth.

The Summer Splash
SERVES 2-3

Ingredients:
3 tablespoons basil, chopped
1 ½ cup blueberries
2 Pinches cayenne pepper
½ lime
5 cups watermelon, diced

Directions:
Add all ingredients to juicer and juice.

The Apple Smoothie
SERVES 4

Ingredients:
1 cup coconut water
1 cup kale
1 cup baby spinach
1 ½ Fuji apples, cored
⅛ teaspoon cinnamon
⅛ teaspoon nutmeg
1 cup ice
Dash of flaxseed or chia seeds (optional)

Directions:
Add all of the ingredients to a blender and blend until smooth.

The Green Melon & Spinach Smoothie
SERVES 4

Ingredients:
1 ½ cups unsweetened coconut milk drink
4 cups baby spinach
1 frozen banana
1 ½ cups honeydew melon, cubed
1 cup ice (optional)

Directions:
Add all of the ingredients to a blender and blend until smooth.

Energy-Boosting Juices

The Clean Green Smoothie
SERVES 4

Ingredients:

1½ cups unsweetened almond milk

1 cup kale

2 cups baby spinach

1 teaspoon green superfood or spirulina

1 ½ frozen bananas

3 teaspoons fresh ginger

2 tablespoons almond butter

1 cup ice

Directions:
Add all of the ingredients to a blender and blend until smooth.

The Green Mango Zing Smoothie
SERVES 3

Ingredients:
1 ¼ cups unsweetened almond milk
2 cups baby spinach
1 cup frozen mango
1 frozen banana
1 teaspoon bee pollen
2 teaspoons spirulina
4 tablespoons (1 scoop) protein powder

Directions:
Add all of the ingredients to a blender and blend until smooth.

The Whatchamacallit Smoothie
SERVES 2

Ingredients:
3 organic carrots, scrubbed
5 cups baby spinach
1 cup fresh pineapple
1 large cucumber
⅛ teaspoon cinnamon

Directions:
Add all of the ingredients to a blender except the cinnamon. Blend until smooth. Whisk in the cinnamon.

The Mango-Kale Kicker
SERVES 1

Ingredients:
3 cups baby spinach
1 cup kale
½ ripe mango, pitted, sliced
1 cup coconut water

Directions:
Add all of the ingredients except the coconut water. Juice. Whisk in the coconut water.

The Carrot Dandelion Detox
SERVES 1

Ingredients:
½ pound organic carrots, scrubbed
2 cups baby spinach
¾ cup dandelion greens
1 tablespoon fresh ginger
½ Fuji apple

Directions:
Add all of the ingredients to juicer, being sure to alternate between ingredients.

The Spicy Ginger Pineapple
SERVES 1-2

Ingredients:
¾ cup fresh pineapple
3 cups baby spinach
1 tablespoon fresh ginger
1 medium cucumber

Directions:
Add all of the ingredients to a juicer and juice. Optional, whisk in cinnamon.

The Green Pineapple Punch Smoothie
SERVES 4

Ingredients:
1 ½ cups unsweetened coconut milk drink
2 cups baby spinach
1 frozen banana
1 cup fresh pineapple
1 teaspoon spirulina
1 teaspoon bee pollen
1 cup ice

Directions:
Add all of the ingredients to a blender and blend until smooth.

The Cinnamon-Almond Smoothie
SERVES 2

Ingredients:
1 cup unsweetened almond milk
1 frozen banana
1 teaspoon cinnamon
1 tablespoon maca powder
2 tablespoons almond butter
1 cup ice

Directions:
Add all of the ingredients to a blender and blend until smooth.

The Acai Super Smoothie
SERVES 3

Ingredients:
2 100-gram acai frozen berry packs (by Sambazon)
2 cup baby spinach
1 frozen banana
1 ¼ cups coconut water
1 tablespoon spirulina
1 tablespoon green superfood

Directions:
Add all of the ingredients to a blender and blend until smooth.

The Chocolate Boost Smoothie
SERVES 2

Ingredients:

1 ¼ cups unsweetened almond milk

1 cup baby spinach

1 tablespoon green superfood

1 tablespoon spirulina

1 frozen banana

2 tablespoons unsweetened cocoa powder

4 tablespoons (1 scoop) protein powder

1 teaspoon bee pollen (optional)

1 teaspoon probiotics powder (optional)

1 cup ice

Directions:
Add all of the ingredients to a blender and blend until smooth.

The Superb Hemp Smoothie
SERVES 2

Ingredients:
1 cup coconut almond milk
1 cup baby spinach
1 tablespoon green superfood
½ frozen banana
2 cups frozen blueberries
2 tablespoons hemp protein powder
1 tablespoon spirulina
1 teaspoon hempseed oil (optional)

Directions:
Add all of the ingredients to a blender and blend until smooth.

The Green Mango Smoothie
SERVES 4

Ingredients:
2½ cups unsweetened almond milk
1 ½ cups kale
3cups frozen mango
1 tablespoon spirulina

Directions:
Add all of the ingredients to a blender and blend until smooth.

The Revitalizing Peanut Butter Smoothie
SERVES 2

Ingredients:
1 cup unsweetened almond milk
1 frozen banana
½ cup pineapple
2 tablespoons natural peanut butter
2 tablespoons maca root powder
1 cup ice

Directions:
Add all of the ingredients to a blender and blend until smooth.

Low-Cal Juices

The Green Cucumber
SERVES 1

Ingredients:
1 large cucumber
¼ Fuji or Granny Smith apple
¼ cup fresh parsley
1 tablespoon lemon juice (optional)

Directions:
Juice all of the ingredients except the lemon juice. Whisk in the lemon juice last.

The Spinach Pineapple Smoothie
SERVES 2-4

Ingredients:
1 cup unsweetened almond milk
3 cups baby spinach
1 cup fresh pineapple (or frozen pineapple)
1 cup ice

Directions:
Add all ingredients to a blender and blend until smooth.

The Minty Cantaloupe Refresher Smoothie
SERVES 3

Ingredients:
1 cup unsweetened almond milk
2 cup cantaloupe melon
3 tablespoons fresh mint
1 cup ice

Directions:
Add all ingredients to a blender and blend until smooth.

The Ginger-Vanilla Zen Smoothie
SERVES 3

Ingredients:
1 cup unsweetened almond milk
1 frozen banana
½ pear
1 tablespoon fresh ginger, grated
1 teaspoon organic vanilla extract
½ cup Greek or coconut yogurt
1 ½ cups ice

Directions:
Add all ingredients to a blender and blend until smooth.

Juice of a Salad
SERVES 1

Ingredients:
1 cucumber
1 lemon
1 medium scallion
1 handful parsley
½ medium sweet red pepper
3 small whole tomatoes

Directions:
Add all of the ingredients to a juicer and juice.

The Peachy Green Smoothie
SERVES 4

Ingredients:
1½ cups unsweetened almond milk
2 cups baby spinach
2 cups frozen, organic peaches
½ Bartlett pear, cored
1 teaspoon bee pollen (optional)
1 tablespoon green superfood

Directions:
Add all ingredients to a blender and blend until smooth.

The Green Apple Cleanser
SERVES 2

Ingredients:
3 cups baby spinach
2 cups kale
2 medium cucumbers
½ cup fresh pineapple
1 Fuji apple

Directions:
Add all ingredients to a blender and blend until smooth.

The Pumpkin Pineapple Smoothie
SERVES 4

Ingredients:
1 ½ cups unsweetened coconut almond milk
2 cups baby spinach
1 Bartlett pear, cored
¾ cup fresh pineapple
¾ cup organic pumpkin puree
¼ teaspoon pumpkin spice
1 cup ice

Directions:
Add all ingredients to a blender and blend until smooth.

The Soothing Grapefruit
SERVES 1

Ingredients:
4 organic carrots, scrubbed
½ large cucumber
1 pink grapefruit, peeled
1 teaspoon ginger

Directions:
Add all ingredients to a juicer and juice.

Carrot and Ginger on the Green
SERVES 1

Ingredients:
5 cups baby spinach
3 organic carrots, scrubbed
½ Bartlett pear, cored
1 tablespoon ginger

Directions:
Add all ingredients to a juicer and juice.

The Peachy Kale
SERVES 1

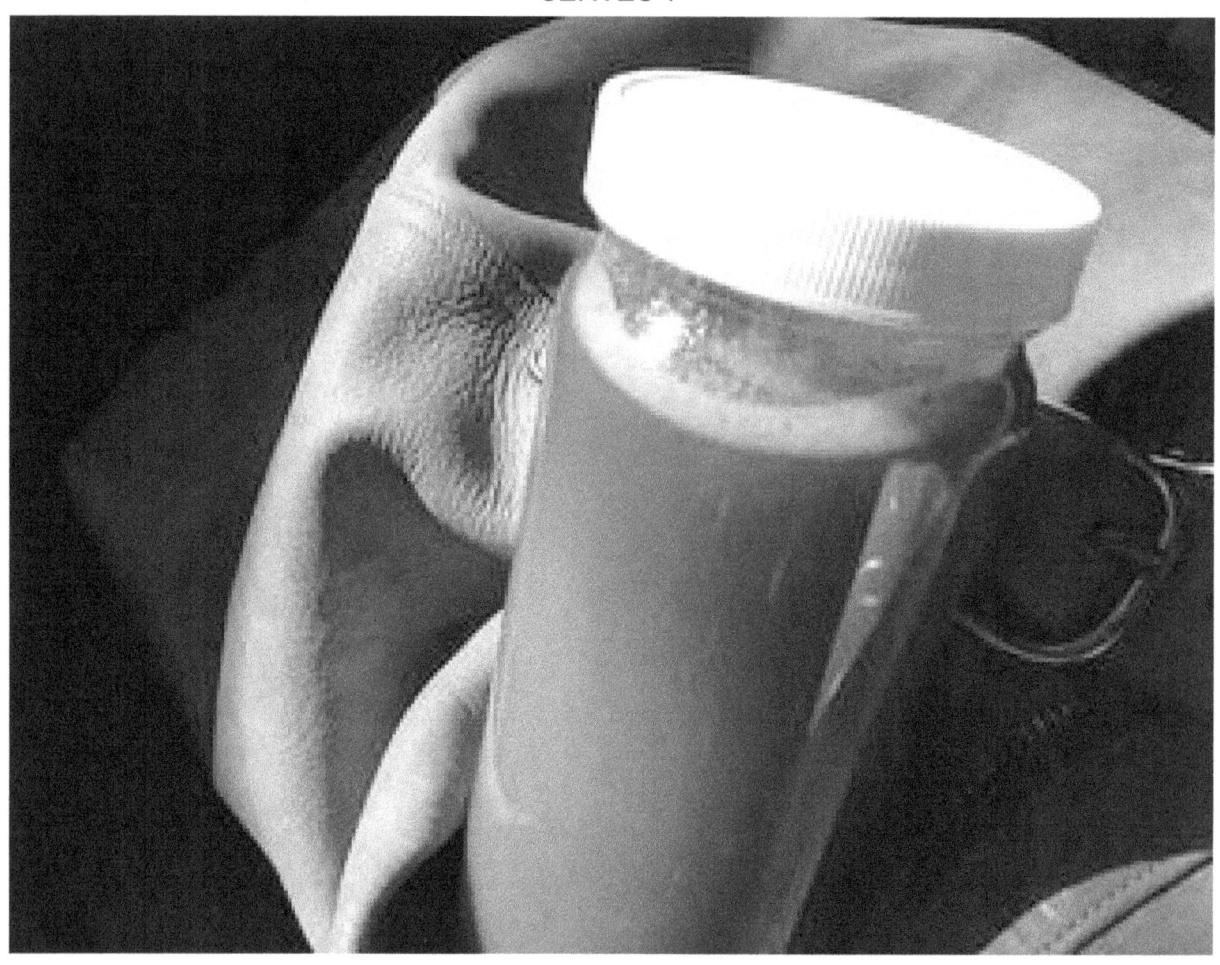

Ingredients:
1 cup kale
4 cups baby spinach
¾ fresh peach, pitted
½ medium cucumber

Directions:
Add all ingredients to a juicer and juice.

Clear Skin Juices & Smoothies

Carrot Cake Juice
SERVES 2 (small glasses)

Ingredients:
4 cups baby spinach
1 pound bag of organic carrots, scrubbed
½ Fuji apple
¼ teaspoon ground cinnamon
¼ teaspoon pumpkin spice

Directions:
Add all of the ingredients to a juicer except the cinnamon and pumpkin spice. Add to glass and whisk in cinnamon and pumpkin spice.

The Glowing Kale
SERVES 1

Ingredients:
3 cups kale
1 cup baby spinach
½ Bosc pear, cored
1 cucumber
¼ lemon

Directions:
Add all of the ingredients to a juicer and juice, being sure to alternate ingredients.

The Minty Cucumber Coconut Purifier
SERVES 2

Ingredients:
1 medium cucumber
3 cups baby spinach
¼ Fuji apple
5 tablespoons fresh mint
1 cup coconut water.

Directions
Add all of the ingredients except coconut water to juicer and juice. Add the coconut water and whisk well.

The Peachy Ginger
SERVES 2

Ingredients:
2 cups kale
5 cups baby spinach
1 teaspoon fresh ginger
¾ peach, pitted
¼ cup coconut water

Directions:
Add all of the ingredients except the coconut water to juicer and juice. Whisk in the coconut water.

The Sweet Peach Booster Smoothie
SERVES 4

Ingredients:
2 ½ cups unsweetened almond milk
½ frozen banana
¾ cup sweet potato puree, or steamed sweet potatoes
3 cups frozen, organic peaches
¼ teaspoon pumpkin spice
¼ teaspoon nutmeg
¼ teaspoon cinnamon
4 tablespoons (1 scoop) protein powder (optional)

Directions:
Add all of the ingredients to a blender and blend until smooth.

Pumpkin on the Green Smoothie
SERVES 3

Ingredients:
1 ½ cups unsweetened almond milk
2 cups baby spinach
1 Bartlett pear, cored
½ frozen banana
¾ cup pumpkin puree
2 tablespoons protein powder (optional)

Directions:
Add all of the ingredients to a blender and blend until smooth.

The Pumpkin Pie Smoothie
SERVES 4

Ingredients:
1 ½ cups unsweetened almond milk
2 frozen bananas
1 Bartlett pear, cored
½ cup pumpkin puree
1 tablespoon grated ginger
¼ teaspoon pumpkin spice
1 cup ice

Directions:
Add all of the ingredients to a blender and blend until smooth.

The Super Skin Cleanser Smoothie
SERVES 2

Ingredients:
1 cup coconut water
1 cucumber
2 cups watermelon
1 cup ice

Directions:
Add all of the ingredients to a blender and blend until smooth.

The Blueberry Bliss Smoothie
SERVES 4

Ingredients:
1 cup coconut water
1cup organic baby spinach
1 Bartlett pear, halved, cored
2 cups frozen blueberries
2tablespoons lemon juice
1 teaspoon lemon zest

Directions:
Add all of the ingredients to a blender and blend until smooth.

The Hydrating Cucumber Pear Smoothie
SERVES 2

Ingredients:
1 cup unsweetened coconut milk beverage
1 cup baby spinach
1 Bartlett pear, cored
½ large cucumber
1 tablespoon shredded, sweet coconut (optional)
1 cup ice

Directions:
Add all of the ingredients to a blender and blend until smooth.

The Raspberry Beauty Potion Smoothie
SERVES 2

Ingredients:

1 ½ cups coconut water

2 cups baby spinach

1 cup organic frozen raspberries

1 teaspoon fresh lavender (or ¼ teaspoon dried)

2 tablespoons resveratrol

1 cup ice

Directions:

Add all of the ingredients to a blender and blend until smooth.

The Cucumber Cleansing Smoothie
SERVES 3

Ingredients:

½ cup coconut water

1 cup coconut-almond milk blend

1 medium cucumber, sliced

½ Bartlett pear, cored

3 tablespoons fresh mint

1 ½ cups ice

Directions:

Add all of the ingredients in a blender and blend until smooth.

The Avocado Mango Smoothie
SERVES 4

Ingredients:
1 cup water
1 orange, peeled
2 cups baby spinach
1 ripe avocado, peeled and seeded
½ cup fresh pineapple
1 cup frozen mango

Directions:
Add all of the ingredients to a blender and blend until smooth.

Brain-booster Juices & Smoothies

The Romaine Coconut Smoothie
SERVES 4

Ingredients:
2 cups unsweetened coconut milk beverage
1 cup romaine lettuce
1 frozen banana
2 tablespoons almond butter
3 tablespoon sweetened coconut shavings
1 tablespoon flaxseed meal
4 teaspoons organic vanilla extract
1 cup ice

Directions:
Add all of the ingredients to a blender and blend until smooth.

The Green Coconut Smoothie
SERVES 2

Ingredients:
1 cup unsweetened coconut milk drink
2 cups baby spinach
2 tablespoons green superfood
2 tablespoons almond butter
¼ teaspoon cinnamon
1 tablespoon hemp seed
1 cup ice

Directions:
Add all of the ingredients to a blender and blend until smooth.

The Green Diva Smoothie
SERVES 4

Ingredients:
1½ cups unsweetened almond milk
2 cups baby spinach
2 cups kale
1 ½ cups pineapple
1 large cucumber
1 tablespoon ground flaxseed
4 tablespoons (1 scoop) protein powder
2 cups ice

Directions:
Add all of the ingredients to a blender and blend until smooth.

The Happy Chia Smoothie
SERVES 2

Ingredients:
1 ½ cups unsweetened coconut milk beverage
3 cups baby spinach
1 frozen banana
2tablespoons almond butter
3 tablespoons chia seeds
2 teaspoons organic vanilla extract
½ cup ice

Directions:
Add all of the ingredients to a blender and blend until smooth.

The Chocolate Chia Smoothie
SERVES 2

Ingredients:
1 ¼ cups unsweetened almond milk
2 cups kale
1 frozen banana
2 dried dates, pitted
2 tablespoons chia seeds
2 tablespoons unprocessed, unsweetened cocoa powder
1 cup ice

Directions:
Add all of the ingredients to a blender and blend until smooth.

The Green Avocado Peach Smoothie
SERVES 4

Ingredients:
1cup unsweetened almond milk
2 cups baby spinach
2cups frozen organic peaches
1 teaspoon flaxseed oil
1 ripe avocado, pitted

Directions:
Add all of the ingredients to a blender and blend until smooth.

The Green Almond Butter Pumpkin Smoothie
SERVES 2

Ingredients:
1 cup unsweetened almond milk
2 cups baby spinach
¾ cup organic pumpkin puree
2 tablespoons flaxseed meal
2 tablespoons almond butter
½ teaspoon pumpkin spice
1 cup ice (optional)

Directions:
Add all of the ingredients to a blender and blend until smooth.

The Creamy Green Shake Smoothie
SERVES 2

Ingredients:
1 cup unsweetened almond milk
2 cups baby spinach
1 cup kale
1 frozen banana
3 dried dates, pitted
1 tablespoon chia seeds
1 teaspoon flaxseed oil
1 tablespoon organic vanilla extract

Directions:
Add all of the ingredients to a blender and blend until smooth.

The Green Tea Cleansing Smoothie
SERVES 2

Ingredients:
1 ¼ cups unsweetened almond milk
1 cup baby spinach
1 cup kale
1 frozen banana
2teaspoons matcha green tea powder
1 tablespoon chia seeds
1 teaspoon flaxseed oil
1 teaspoon maple syrup (optional)
½ cup ice (optional)

Directions:
Add all of the ingredients to a blender and blend until smooth.

Calming Juices & Smoothies

The Lavender Honeydew
SERVES 2

Ingredients:
3 cups baby spinach
1 cup honeydew melon
2 tablespoons fresh lavender
1 cup coconut water
½ cup water

Directions:
Add all ingredients to juicer except the coconut water. Juice. Whisk in the coconut water.

The Lavender Cucumber Refresher Smoothie
SERVES 2

Ingredients:
1 cup unsweetened almond milk
1 cup cucumber
1 tablespoon fresh lavender (or 1 teaspoon dried)
1 cup Greek or coconut yogurt
1 tablespoon mint
1 cup ice

Directions:
Add all ingredients to a blender and blend until smooth.

The Basil Honeydew
SERVES 2

Ingredients:
1 cup honeydew melon
3 cups baby spinach
¼ cup fresh basil
¼ cup fresh mint
1 large cucumber

Directions:
Add all ingredients to a juicer and juice.

The Calming Melon Smoothie
SERVES 3

Ingredients:
½ cup coconut water
1cup honeydew melon
2 cups baby spinach
2tablespoons fresh mint 1
teaspoon fresh lavender
1 cup ice

Directions:
Add all ingredients to a blender and blend until smooth.

The Trifecta: Mint, Melon, Mango Smoothie
SERVES 3

Ingredients:
1 cup coconut water
1 cup frozen mango
2 cups baby spinach
1 cup honeydew melon
¼ cup fresh mint
1 ½ cups ice

Directions:
Add all ingredients to a blender and blend until smooth.

The Chocolate Avocado Diva Smoothie
SERVES 2

Ingredients:
1 ¼ cups unsweetened almond milk
1 ripe avocado, pitted
1 frozen banana
2tablespoons dark unsweetened cocoa powder
2 teaspoons agave nectar (if you must)
1 cup ice

Directions:
Add all ingredients to a blender and blend until smooth.

The Calming Vanilla Pear Smoothie
SERVES 2

Ingredients:

1 cup unsweetened almond milk

1 frozen banana

1 Bartlett pear, cored

1 tablespoon organic vanilla extract

1 cup ice

Directions:

Add all ingredients to a blender and blend until smooth.

The Green Blueberry Smoothie
SERVES 4

Ingredients:
2 cups unsweetened almond milk
2 cups kale
1 frozen banana
1 cup frozen blueberries
1 tablespoon fresh lavender (or 1 teaspoon dried lavender)
1 teaspoon bee pollen
1 tablespoon green superfood

Directions:
Add all ingredients to a blender and blend until smooth.

The Honeydew Mint Smoothie
SERVES 2

Ingredients:
1 cup unsweetened coconut-almond milk
1 cup honeydew melon
3 tablespoons fresh mint leaves
1 tablespoon bee pollen
1 teaspoon probiotics/acidophilus
1 ½ cups ice

Directions:
Add all ingredients to a blender and blend until smooth.

The Calm Green Pineapple
SERVES 2 (small glasses)

Ingredients:
2 cups baby spinach
1 large cucumber
¼ cup fresh pineapple
1 tablespoon fresh ginger.

Directions:
Add all ingredients to a juicer and juice.

The Chocolate Peanut Butter Shake Smoothie
SERVES 2

Ingredients:
1 cup unsweetened almond milk
2 cups baby spinach
1 frozen banana
2 tablespoons natural peanut butter
2 tablespoons unsweetened cocoa powder
4 tablespoons (1 scoop) protein powder
1 cup ice

Directions:
Add all ingredients to a blender and blend until smooth.

The Green Pineapple & Cinnamon Smoothie
SERVES 4

Ingredients:
1 ½ cups unsweetened coconut-almond milk
2 cups baby spinach
1 frozen banana
1 cup fresh pineapple
½ teaspoon cinnamon

Directions:
Add all ingredients to a blender and blend until smooth.

The Ginger Carrot
SERVES 2

Ingredients:
1 pound organic carrots, scrubbed
1 tablespoons fresh ginger
1 large cucumber

Directions:
Add all ingredients to a juicer and juice.

The Tart Pear Lemonade
SERVES 2

Ingredients:
3 cups baby spinach
½ lemon
1 Bartlett pear, cored
½ cup coconut water
½ cup water

Directions:
Juice all ingredients except the coconut water and water. After juicing, whisk in the waters.

The Super Green Lemonade
SERVES 1

Ingredients:
5 cups baby spinach
1 cup honeydew melon
½ lemon, plus 1 tablespoon lemon juice
½ medium cucumber
1 teaspoon spirulina powder

Directions:
Add all ingredients to juicer except the spirulina powder and lemon juice. After juicing, whisk in the spirulina and lemon juice.

The Toasted Coconut Strawberry Smoothie
SERVES 4

Ingredients:
2 cups unsweetened coconut milk drink
2 cups organic frozen strawberries
2 tablespoons toasted coconut shavings (divided)
1 tablespoon lemon juice
1 tablespoon spirulina (optional)
1 teaspoon bee pollen.

Directions:
Add ingredients with one tablespoon of the coconut to a blender and blend until smooth. Using the remaining coconut, toast in upper third for a few minutes at 350 degrees. Cool and top smoothie.

The Kicker
SERVES 1

Ingredients:
1 head romaine lettuce
3 organic carrots, scrubbed
1 tablespoon fresh ginger
¼ tablespoon lemon juice

Directions:
Add all ingredients to a juicer and juice except the lemon juice. Whisk in the lemon juice.

The Super Blueberry Smoothie
SERVES 3

Ingredients:
1 ½ cups coconut water
3 cups baby spinach
1 tablespoon green superfood
1 frozen banana
1 cup frozen blueberries
1 teaspoon bee pollen
1 tablespoon spirulina

Directions:
Add all ingredients to a blender and blend until smooth.

The Vitamin C Smoothie
SERVES 2

Ingredients:
½ cup coconut water
1 cup frozen strawberries
2 oranges, peeled
1 cup Greek or coconut yogurt
1 tablespoon bee pollen
1 teaspoon probiotics
1 cup ice

Directions:
Add all ingredients to a blender and blend until smooth.

The Super Strawberry Smoothie
SERVES 3

Ingredients:
2 ½ cups unsweetened coconut almond milk
1 cup baby spinach
1 frozen banana
2cups frozen strawberries
1 teaspoon probiotics
1 teaspoon bee pollen

Directions:
Add all ingredients to a blender and blend until smooth.

The Hangover Smoothie
SERVES 2

Ingredients:
1cup unsweetened almond milk
1 cup kale
2 frozen bananas
1 cup frozen strawberries
1 cup frozen blueberries
1 tablespoon fennel seeds
1 cup ice

Directions:
Add all ingredients to a blender and blend until smooth.

The Green Ginger OJ
SERVES 1

Ingredients:
½ large cucumber
3 cups baby spinach
1 orange, peeled
1 tablespoon ginger

Directions:
Add all ingredients to a juicer and juice.

The Berry Goddess Smoothie
SERVES 3

Ingredients:
1 ½ cups coconut water
1 cup baby spinach
1 cup frozen blueberries
1 cup frozen strawberries
2 teaspoons spirulina
1 tablespoon probiotics/acidophilus
2 tablespoons resveratrol

Directions:
Add all ingredients to a blender and blend until smooth.

Disclaimer Statement

All information and content contained in this book are provided solely for general information and reference purposes. S.S. Publishing LLC Limited makes no statement, representation, warranty or guarantee as to the accuracy, reliability or timeliness of the information and content contained in this Book.

Neither SSP Limited or the author of this book nor any of its related company accepts any responsibility or liability for any direct or indirect loss or damage (whether in tort, contract or otherwise) which may be suffered or occasioned by any person howsoever arising due to any inaccuracy, omission, misrepresentation or error in respect of any information and content provided by this book (including any third-party books.